Praise th

Praise the Unburied

by Clara Burghelea

First published in Ireland in 2021 by Chaffinch Press

Chaffinch Press

ISBN: 978-1-8384025-5-6

'Every poem is the story of itself.'

Duende, Tracy K. Smith

Contents

Ghostification

A Tincture for Wounds

How to turn poetry prompt #5 into girl power

Self-medicating with St John's Wort

Some Kind of Love

Ghostification

Confession

A mother wound lives under the skin.
Undone at first, throbbing less in time.

It dwells between the ribs, under the left
breast, the one she lost to cancer. At night,

you catch yourself thinking the dearth isn't
real. An abundance of gifts fills your days.

From doilies she crocheted on the living
room table to teaching you to coddle perfect

eggs that taste like fresh love, the way your
daughter smiles down into her sweater, comes

back sucking up the frayed collar. The idle hugs
your son gives to Seven, the husky, while feeding

him French fries in the rosy afterglow of dinner,
the breath of late summer on his cheeks, the heart's

hungry atrium begging for the day to linger, young
love to sop into the bread that it is us. Always rising.

Portrait of my mother in the middle of things

The way she relished in sitting with daily life,
peeling potatoes for hours in a row, then doing
her nails burgundy red. Forgetting is essential,
she said as she dunked her fingers into hot water
only to come out perfectly polished, no smudge
whatsoever. She then flaked garlic cloves, sheer
skins piling up under her humming touch. She would
get a stamp on things - laundry, dishes, number of hugs,
night shifts, cigarette smoking, morning snuggles, and
everything by twos. Children, painkillers, bruises, shopping
bags, don't sees and cant's, dream skins shed down the cold
tiles, crocheting needles, blood-spoored pies, yesterdays
and tomorrows twinned in always. Wound, loving its hurt.

Ghostification

The small bedroom in my parents 'apartment,
my mother, by the window, watering the plants.

Her back cracks like an old chest as she stretches
to prune the ficus. A green-god structure bending

under her apt fingers. Behind the curtains, a tissue
of cloud. Light, a spill of uncut diamonds.

You don't know yet this is going to be the best day
in a long row of choked-up blues, tinking

and frogging until there is nothing left to mend.
Before you pack a small suitcase filled with

bruises and go down into the moist November,
you'll suddenly recall the ficus needs watering.

Ode to the 80s scrapbooks

We called them oracole as if they could tell the future
when all we wanted was to be seen in that moment.

All shin and burning eyes, best-friend necklaces and
oversized sweaters our mothers knitted while doing

extra night shifts at the chemical plant that fed and kept
half a town and what a town that was. Too large to

contain whispers that made trees move on their inside
and then, too small to matter when Ceausescu visited

on August 23, 1986, and we waited half a day in the sun,
churning stomachs and scorched ears, to sing our hearts out

to multiubitul tovarăş, and the power failure at the chemical
plant screwed up phone lines and we were never told he would

go straight to Sibiu, his son's residence town, and 3400 kids,
all braids and cravate roşii, dreamt under the cobalt skies, stems

of their hearts stitched together. The rest of that summer tiptoed
into our blocks of flats as we lay on our bellies on the cold

linoleum. Cutting and pasting flori, fete, filme sau băieți
in our secret books, dripping wax on folded scented pages

where secrets stained like bruises, then swaped them while
waiting in line for bread, always super careful not to lose

our ration cards. We would not yet miss the imploding youth
in our bones, the teen-thin thirst in our foraging fingers.

.

Mothering

Before Tuesday rolls into Thursday,
I am all kinds of weather, mostly drizzle.
Mornings have a way of sneaking up,
burnt toast and sticky jam, milk on tiles.
By noon, love comes in Tupperware boxes,
more fits and starts. Headaches flutter like
broken-winged butterflies, worn body eager
to crawl back into pupa at nightfall. Behind
closed eyes, I dream of lavish maunderings,
bold, scissor-slit poems at every street corner.

Limenas, half-light

The Greek sun dissolved
into violet loose glitter,
the buttering sea
motherly brushing my feet.
By dark, I'll become a ghost,
all foam and salty limbs.

My therapist asks me to write down ten things my mother loved

To walk her sturdy calves in high-heeled
shoes her husband forbade to parade.

To put on red lipstick, smoke at sunset,
and rule over peeled garlic cloves.

To turn love into soup, each semolina
dumpling easier than a summer kiss.

To keep an apple soap bar in the drawer,
forget about mixing lye for cloth washing.

To drink real coffee, never nechezol, in pretty
cups held by manicured ladylike hands.

To call us balls of fluff, then huddle together,
never looking the rusty radiator in the eye.

To read good books, wrapped in Scânteia,
on the bus, third shifting to her dusty lab beakers.

To smell our sickly-sweet sleep smell off our napes,
call us sweaty chickens for eighteen summers in a row.

To blow away fever spells with the quick staccato of her
voice, her own gaze burning longer into the long night.

To linger on, inside her handwritten recipe notebook,
my son’s left cheek dimple, spark in every cruel sunrise.

The hues of April blues in Long Island

The feeble budding leaves,
the purple of the hyacinth
and in the sky, Canadian geese
crying spring. I wonder if

my missing mother could smell
this foreign life, these lonesome
stances of earth's splendor
when you are allowed to feel grand,

much as you stand small,
deliver yourself unto the universe
and succumb to its lush of meanings.
Grief cannot keep the world from spinning.

Needle threading towards reparation

I am looking at us from the inside,
my forehead alive with questions,

the wind's nudge on my sunken shoulders.
These days, I live between spring riot

and your smell swarming the air. Except
it's been weeks since I last thought of you

in a way that is inviting, trusting the hours
that pass to help me shake off any fleck

of memory, little shreds of orange pith,
neither to be eaten, nor thrown away.

I haven't thought about my mother in months

just me, these days in every window's reflection,
same hair, different way of wearing the face.
My mother's, thick with febrile caution. Mine,
falling into itself, a millipede kind of movement.
For a long time, pain lived in the zippered pocket
of my purse, ruffling its silver scales. Every time
an alone spell came to an end, her image would
fall and accumulate without notice, a residue
of grief, and those flakes of skin hardened even
more, until my brains cratered and I would sleep
for days, numb dawns on a string, vacant flesh.
Among the living, I stride with others, lumpy fish.

White-night odes

The mothers we carry, the mothers we crave
are everywhere but where we need them.
In the soft soil, the hardy grass, the muscled
force of grief at dawn or maybe is it at night,
when under light sheets, next to the man that
stirs the flesh, tangled and dark, the soul lays
awake. At wee hours, mothers descend into the
sweaty rooms to scold and soothe alike, draped
in the weight of the previous day, unloading
dreams into our veins, pointing to the places
it hurts most, the crooked seams, the radiating
lines, the petty late-night thoughts, the yearning
hearts, in a word, everything that stays unnamed,
yet throbbing. Next, their peeping-tom breath
over our shoulders as we make breakfast or beds,
dust off furniture or broth our ways through
the remainder of the week, poems as lungs, charring
our throats, no mouth to spit them out. Mary on
the wall keeps a vigil eye on our daily unnecessaries
and we'd rather give ourselves in small-tied bites
to the devil if ligament, sacrum, tendon could rest.

What occasionally makes sense

I might be my mother's mother for all I know.
Sharp-tongued and making things up as they come along.

Words, grape juice, meals. Tonguing her teeth before
chopping onion to make ostropel de pui cu mămăliguță.

To be eaten around the three-legged wooden table,
our backs bent over the steaming pot. In the plum tree

in front of the summer kitchen, a magpie eyeing the little
chicks roaming along the red hen. Some inviting promise

in their rousing yellow and the bird knows it. She hungers
to name it. This craving that fills the tender July air, still

with flavors and lures. We are all women of appetites
in this house. Grandma makes must every fall, crushing

dark and white grapes by hand. We drink it the next day,
sediment and froth, and eat pastramă with it. My mother

cuts the mutton in thin slices, rubs salt, pepper, chili
and thyme against it. Rolls it up, keeps it cool for days

in a row. Then it hangs in the afumătoare where the aroma
tingles my nostrils and gives me goose bumps. Later, the three

of us breaking bread as evening comes chattering down
and this very alphabet of love blooms into our veins.

Every other morning, I crave to smell my mother's smell,
all honeycomb, vinegar and exhaustion. The crook of her neck

is where this intoxication begins, every purple first light,
for the next thirty years. I will then wake up to a mouthful

of needles whose wholeness won't stay put, much as I bleed
my way through their eyes. Slivers of past conversations, gestures

and wouldas nest under every fold of skin. Vast tomorrows lay
ahead, jottings of poems scratch at every white corner and not even

a daughter can give me back the pleasure of the mouth, the seduction
of endless noons filled with albă-ca-zăpada, salată de vinete,

the in-between hugs and shared layers of fatigue, natter and laughter.
Except my daughter wears your calves the same way, and grandma

reminds me every Saturday when I visit of the way hunger never
apologizes and that there are no rooms in our bodies without ghosts.

A Tincture for Wounds

Anatomy of a single sun's day

Coffee, black enough to matter, April sun brushing
against the wood of the shutters, jasmine vine coiled

around the string, the promise of the star flower
still cradled in the pod. The din of love, gathering,

receding, returning. In the slaty-blue eye of the jay
up the cherry tree, the torturing green of the grass,

the numb flow of the same yesterdays and tomorrows
caught in time's toothless mouth. Inside, something

hurling itself against the grieving bones, ready
to rewild half the earth. Who would break the spell?

Your lips, a pellet of rage, some sigh floating around,
the violent summer that will lend itself to us, only

to slip through our hungry fingers. Between leaving
and staying, behold this small patch of slumber.

Halves of things

A bruise down the thigh or sinking
teeth into another flesh. A ring of sky,
or the deafening storm. Dreaming

of coffee all my life, then hives.
Obsessed with soft leeches,
choking at the sight of blood.

To have and to hold, otherwise
easy with the in-betweens. Ink
sliding on paper, then softly barren.

Lying on the floor with you,
naming all secrets, or tending
to the inner workings of my day.

Angst, hedged beneath my left breast,
like a bone. Ghosts of fingernails.

In the suburbs

At night, bodies unfold their pretty scars
and souls start rattling their cages.
Morning, always fresh and unhurried.
Midday is to be lived within itself,
good food, tempered laughter,
a bottle of Amarone.
There is an aristocratic cadence
in the way time punctures the day.

Under eyelids

Chia pudding to soften the day,
black coffee to bear its weight.
Melody Gardot on repeat, smooth
like Persian rug. Eyelids of velvet.
On the chair, a dress bought on
consignment. Another woman's

lifetime of Octobering, woven
inside the silky red. The half-breaths.
Down the street, the bold steam of pork
dumplings. Then, a mouthful of birds.
Before the two-kid commotion erupts
and the day peels off like dry shallot,

heart pounds out a whisper. Just, linger
on, right into the folds of these high dreams.

Contretemps

Light hauls me out of bed, Greek sun
piercing the old shutters. A slipper,

soft as a creature, lies at the wooden
foot of the bed. Your scent lingers

on my breath like a promise. Like
oozing sand. The cry of a ghost bird

slays the air. Limbs stretch the length
of a wall in China. A persimmon in half

on the wrinkled table. Its fork-shaped seed
smiles a mild winter, claims the fruit seller.

It is worth a bite. Outside the window,
the postcard home day peels off in slow motion.

Against the teal-smeared wall, old and new
shadows bear their weight in silence.

In undergloom

Draw us family-style nibbling raspberry
fullness, all hue and scent, rustling of silk

and tang against the roof of the mouth.
Fresh from the west corner of the garden,

seeds of spell crushed between teeth,
tongue swollen with longing. Last summer

shadows, smooth as milk-glass before lungs
caught fire. Find forward four empty seats,

ghost breath soaring like fresh kite. Sun,
pulsating medusae limbs across the left wall,

terraformed footprints goodbying by inch.
Resilience in the making. Think sharp teeth

at the end of a fork poking for the soft edges
of things. Unrepentant, the pumiced dawn.

The twenty-year marriage

is mostly about meals. Tonight, we praise
the texture of the tiger bass and the herbs
we brought from Thassos. We share a glass
of crispy, white wine and cover vast territories

in our conversations. You let your fingers graze
on my palm, then nibble on a valerian leaf
from my salad. Some things hang in the air like
heavy fruit. The leaving, this numbness, the shared

silences. Outside the window, guinea pig babies
squeal at the sound of our voices. It took us months
to discover their almost human need: to sleep on
our laps while being stroked, always on a full belly.

Two hearts can ram each other and have desire stir
desire before all gale descends into a mighty calm.

At the villa

At Villa Teresa in Limenas

This talcum-dusted morning, M and S gathered sea
treasures: a small urchin, two crabs, a speckled mussel.
Behind a pinkish stone, they spotted a honeyed anemone.
Let's call it Mona! they cried, asking for approval.
They placed each of their beauties in plastic cups,
on sand beds and filled them with salty water.
They set about trying to teach them the human ways-
move when summoned, swim as told, rejoice upon
seeing their freckled faces. Now what? Now we wait.
A sea will be growing on our little terrace
and we'll have to name it and care for it!
S said with authority. Twelve is all about being right
and unforgiving, a pair of joint eyebrows
to seal the deal. M's eyes filling with tears:
But this is not our home. We cannot leave our sea behind!
A shred of kind pain on his tanned cheeks.
I hold myself behind the lacey curtains. I wish my love
could seam their world and save them from its rage.
A mother's will is bone, each breath perforating the lungs.
M and S rest their foreheads on the plastic cups,
their silhouettes a spell of fabric against the sky's lavender.

Mal de mer

Behind the fissures, salty yearnings.
The ebb and flow healing bouts
of the Ionian. A precise animal,
cutting waves, one breath holding
the next, sand bruises. Air singing
of torpor, secluded scent of the armpits,
worn out by the heaviness of your body
next to mine, the gladdening breeze
of god's lungs over still things.
A batch of turnings and returnings.

Quarantine love

I hear time trickle alongside walls, ghost
fingers prying through the yawning door,
a splotch of red in the tall grass. Lichen
buds sprout inside the creases of the mind.

The thawing of your hunger fills the cheek
of the blue tilt, my eyelids parched with light,
no tongue to smooth away the strips of silence.
Days in fossilized amber, lactic acid surplus

in the hissing of the rested limbs. Lopsided
want cradled in small places - a scab, white
of the eyes, lips of blueberry, map of the face.
This earth is quick with moist cartilages.

A day spent curled around your face

This achy October, heavy fruit thundering
down. In the grass, brown apples, warm scent

of spoil. Clouds smeared half-way across
the treetops. Among rotting sweetness,

in the tall grass, your chest that rises
and sinks unnoticed, my fingers floating

across familiar flesh, getting lost under
the brittle foliage. The way days oxidize,

tiny summer flakes coming off everything.
Who can trust the hours? The ticking two-timing

hands that push us farther away. Hard to imagine
what lies ahead this dangling numbness, light

growing softer, then deafening dark. In between,
bodies plastered to one another, awaiting winter.

A tincture for wounds

Four months and counting, in a freefall, clocking time between
teeth. Silences fat with longing, while August feverishly unfolds
its gifts, from bursting fruit to evenings swathed in violet. This
summer pilfers our open hearts, while we gaze into old maps
where and what countries we could have held into the eyes and
mouths. The Greek sky running out under our twitching eyelids.
The saltiness of the Thassos mornings burning a hole into our
wanting tongues, children 'shrieks into the turquoise waters, you
and I holding breath, the way one listens to something that is
always ending. The ghost of foreign voices surfacing each morning,
smell taunted by ripening flavors, body following the slow mechanics
of the swindling island, allowing us to inhabit a sheer layer of its

abundance, satiating our cravings with more promise of days
to come. Instead, flaky edges of our backyard thinning days.

How to turn poetry prompt #5 into girl power

Ambience of elsewhere

Jeans and turtleneck, then lick cappuccino froth off a
plastic lid. Watch the slick man by the door, cigarette
hanging from pouting lips. Bask in the indulgence of
a warm pretzel. Milk-teeth clouds and a glitter sun
glued to his hair. Fresh mulch to instruct the senses.
At the back of your mind, a poem ready to stain the page.
Between the silent dahlias and hushed dust-mote words,
the day, as éventail plisse. Here we are, awake and awed.

What makes a girl

First, two names, middle one never really used,
except for paperwork. A father's whim.
To remedy strangers' curiosity,
always tell the appalling story
of the dead twin sister.

Essentially, a quiet bird.
A tangled self-other,
a movement out, carrying back within.
Vortex of sorts. A daughter of divorce.
Mother wound, mother womb, unmothered.
Smothered. Ka-boom. Floating by halves.

Basically, an unsung bird,
chirping in coffee stretches, on buzzing nights,
peeling off softly. Read hunt for heart,
praise the unburied, lick the scab, eat the pain.
Stash poems for blood. Ink be thy Lord.
There, you are a queen, peaking at the moon.

Three winks

In morning cold,
sunrays gambol in the air,
birdsong widening the sky.
The window frames
a square of green-smeared light.
Inside, a poem
holding its breath,
a feathery body of flaws.

Girlhood lessons

Before you are exiled by narrative,
make room for your wicked views,
know that perfect happiness is hardly
a match to fleeting instances of awe.
Some gut-wrenching bouts of grief
will follow and life's teachings and
unteachings remain solid gold. Strike
root in things that make your veins
explode, shed something radiant on
each pillow. A woman's clavicle is
bound to spur the blood and birth a
poem. Beware of hands willing to clip
the moon, legs burning with fever and
the wear-and-tear memory of stale love.
Turn a blind eye to the sad taste of this
spring and look the other three seasons
straight in the eye before you thrust your
greedy teeth into their abundance.

A revision of the self

Begins in the lines and creases
of stanzas, faces, pencil stubs.
There is an inchoate throbbing,
a flowering space asking for alteration.

Feels like pressing curd through cloth,
the inherent softness of the solids,
its pungent flavor, the generous juices.
To be in want for word pains the fingers.

Stands an accolade in the scoop of the day,
a scrim of light, then perhaps too much dark,
the foreboding thought- women do not child,
much as a poem's backbone milks you dry.

Of forgotten tastes

Pressed against the open window,
trees thick with vibrant green.
On the pavement, two women
bicker, arms glistening with sweat.
Cascading voices flood the kitchen.
The radio plays August on repeat.
I made chocolate again. Placed it
on a small tray in the bottom freezer,
then ate powdered milk from the box.
I dreamt of ice caps, the maw of a grey sky
and mountains of white. Against the roof
of the mouth, sugary mounds congealed
around the teeth. A taste of easy Sundays
unburied from piles of Romanian snow,
back in 1986, when mother queued all night
for milk that was as scarce as polar bears.
Morning caught us around the rusty radiator,
cocoa mugs and burnt toast, the promise
of this summer's gasp, a sleeveless dress.

Complicities

The hours are to be trusted in the rigor of their length.
As the day wears on, skin flakes mark your absence.
The saturated air, then drumbeats of foreign light.
The other day, I found your slender book of poems
on a back shelf in The Strand where the ever-smiling
employee took me when I asked for Romanian authors.
I recognized your way of exploring the second language,
domesticating its feral roots. I saw my own struggle
at mastering it. The way language fakes our many deaths,
the right to parade the best scars. It was a kind of love,
I guess, your pain trailing down my hands. On a good day,
I hide down the aisles and let the smell of foreign words
soak up my nostrils before I return to the empty apartment.
Between the snowed-up streets and I, wound as a mound.

Ars Amandi

Sunday afternoon, Limenas beach,
we come across a C-shaped shell.

I run the tips of my fingers across
the edges. This end of September,

a genuflection of fall. A stingless bee
on some withered chrysanthemum.

Before we make this our last station,
place your paraffin palms on the past

few years and squeeze the melting
moments dry. Pegging clothes

to the washing line. Rain glinting behind
the garden. Heath churning the air. Stone

dry womb, your breath silk-stocking
the view. Some blood smearing the rims

of the mother of pearl. Words as symptoms,
marring the gaze, then sea silence all around.

How to turn poetry prompt # 5 into girl power

You can think of your favorite number between five and fifteen.
Then write a poem that has that many lines and takes equal
syllables per line. You might have once tried haikus or tankas,
or take comfort in counting the sparrows perched on red wires,
looking for color symmetry that matches your lopsided
heart, these days skipping beats under layers of sheer gauze,
as you wrangle words, the right words that can soothe, accommodate.
Don't forget to breathe, stay smitten with the world, sashay along
in your red stiletto shoes just because ankles need to be praised
and bodies still sprout in quarantine, under the nib or good hands.
Add up days spent alone, or nights passed awake, take out excess
charges of light, pellets of unexhausted time, madcap guilt.
The remainder is your bare humanity, caught up between
safety pins and beauty on earth so ripe it hurts the teeth numb.
Fifteen is good enough to seduce the blood ink running idle.

A woman/hood

Straw sandal blistering
the ankle, yellow of summer.
A smile that heals,

not knowing it takes
space to grow. Wild women
don't pause their wicked tongues,

yet live against sentences.
Words move like water.
When it is love they shine on,

the day turns into a question.
The rest of the week
closes its eyes to the world,

summer skin grows foreign
pores. Fall becomes a mouth.

To the god on watch

This corner of the afternoon is mine
and the eyes that won't leave me alone.
I am robbing you of the sweet pleasure
of washing the world. In blood, tears
or brine from the Black Sea. I know
a Romanian song about love that tears
the flesh open, a mouth that chars every
syllable, every milky daybreak that tumbles
down choking these October skies bearing
the weight of your smile, a knot of hunger
in every breathing throat and the drizzle
that follows me everywhere. Go blind, now.

Prayer with lullaby eyes

Make room for fresh thoughts,
such as guilt is a hairpin.
To be undone.
Look into the things you love,
rarely the right ones. Give yourself room
to err. Unfurl your winter bones,
ink blood resurges. Call your dead mother,
tell her she is a poem. Then call god a thief
and a wrecker. Pain is hunger,
its roots curling into the flesh.
Tune your ear to its fire. Simmer the tendrils.

Self-medicating with St John's Wort

Madrugada

Pick out a piece of me- a kneecap, a brittle vein,
then a day of asking the way to undo spilled coffee,
warm yourself against things said late at night,
the underside of my chin, cold beer between your legs,
a white moon, taut and urgent, no trick, no trial
just scratch the corners of your nails over my skin.
It is there where the dying begins, the goosebumps
over my ribs won't whisper a thing about the inside storm.
For now, play Yoio Cuesta softly, filling the room with
instances of us going bad, making good. Lay your fat lips,
jitterbugged with sharp-edged kisses, then voice, a saxophone
Sunday cleaning the air in between our bodies.
The insides of my wrists are ready. Let the ink flow.

Hands have twelve lives

My grandmother, caught between Parkinson spells
and sugar fever bouts, tells me her caretaker, dna
Coca, is stealing from her. She went through my
linen and towels, handpicked the pretty ones
and replaced them with these rags. She tilts her
head at a pile of speckled clothes. Burn them,
burn them, she wails. Two hours later, she softly
strokes Coca's hands and calls me little girl,
then gently warns the woman against my sticky
fingers. Last Monday, she waved at some ghost
behind the desk, asked for her pair of crocheted
gloves, spat her denture, then slipped in a kind
of limbo, neither asleep, nor awake, little eyes
bereft of any light. She came back to us, the way
she always does, the little dove, chirpy and ravenous,
gulping her orez cu lapte, feeling the hem of my
skirt, the bare skin, then tenderly touching the air.
Stay close, little girl, God's breath is upon you.

Camera obscura

Plants your mother-in-law tried to kill,
white T-shirt that turns your five o'clock
shadow into flickering dark, bloodshot
eyes that know surplus and absence alike.

Mid-sentence, a raspy Cohen fills the room
and behind the screen, words lay worn out
by the heaviness of your anger. At the world,
its humorless stance, your love for a woman

who's raising another man's pretty children,
yet haunts your wee hours with her moans
and you turn bitter, then soft, that stir in your
plexus dies out before the lark song punctures

the daylight and she, an embrace embraced,
slips again through your fingers, scarring
anew those fleshy palms that will go back
to watering the plants, tongue their dryness.

Called by others to grow upwards

In the car, my son asks me
if his head is oval,
too big for his frame.
Motherness pricks its ears.
The other boys call me a freak.
I sink hands into dress pockets.
His father's cling to the wheel.
Same white knuckles.
I praise the thick eyelashes,
his humor, the left dimple.
His father blames the tallness,
maybe the other boys are envious?
He goes quiet, gazing
outside the window. Nine is a letdown.
The body is preyed, a commodity.
His sigh comes late, a soft breath
that bounces off the roof of the car,
enters his father's teary eyes,
then claws my pounding throat.

Band aid

One time, this guy, an illustrator
I asked to sketch my poems,
showed me a BBC documentary on Bernini.
I sat on a plastic chair in his studio,
in front of a dirty laptop screen. The soothing voice
of Simon Schama filled the stuffed air.
There was something tasteful about his rolling tongue,
like a slice of lime sweetened by a cube of dark sugar.
He spoke of Apollo's desire for Daphne's trembling
flesh and how the purity of the stone
delighted every ignorant heart. I imagined her voice
deeply acquainted with harm. My throat burnt.
The illustrator's hand brushed against my thigh
as he reached to adjust the screen's brightness.
The smooth cream-colored finish of the wall
gleamed in the light, then opened up a toothless mouth.
A portent of stale shame. I jumped to my feet,
the skin behind my naked legs sore,
the taste of an old band aid in my mouth.
Daphne's eyes twitched, pools of hard questions.

Dear Sugar gives late night advice

Be the woman who pulls down
the little mirror in the vizor
before you let him break you

by air drawing a Venn diagram
of how the two of you never overlap
but live within circles of your own.

Add more lipstick on the white lips,
smack them together in confidence,
allowing the Dark Velvet to blend out

towards the edges. Don’t blink, or better,
overdo it. He might hear your ears pop.
Here is the hand, your hand, not his,

feeling the throbbing in your legs
as if they put their mind to it. Press
the sore flesh through the denim

and while doing so, forget to breathe.
The car will shrink and heartbeats
will fog up all windows and somewhere

in the steamy chaos, you will relent
to the numbing and the tingling
and the nauseous choking and there,

long seconds later, the tightly blood
bundle that is your body, will unfold
like a bat, a torn, yet pliable umbrella.

A poem about things I became good at losing

dawns burning in, before I am fleshed and ready,
hairpins in between comfort pillows, coat pockets,
or rainy sidewalks, my mind over raw poems that
birth inside your mouth, slips of paper, car keys,
money, lent books, my mother, my first house, the
compass within, time, hairs, blood, weight, pigment,
memory, sleep, my way in Denver airport, temper a
couple of times, my steps up the snowy hills of Rm.
Vâlcea, mother tongue when birthing lines, two unborn babies, the centripetal force of a hug, wedding
ring while rafting on Salmon River, McCall, Idaho,
the half-said, the unsaid, the evanescent in every
gaze, this languaged body under a pair of deft hands,
a pearl earring down the basin drains in your house,
womb water twice, maiden name, a few inches of
skin, dreams under fresh light, kidney stone, gall
stone, a couple of Tuesdays, a pair of guinea pigs,
soul to flesh, thin to thick, shy hellos to loud exits.

Summer's time

Hands fluttering like birds,
we thread the heat of the day,
children of sand and salt,
ready to gnaw the shores
to their sweet bones.
Across the purple horizon,
sister islands wave seagull arms.

PASS

Pain throbs red as poppy,
the shiny promise of slumber
hidden in the unripe pod.

Body, foreign and numb,
coils like weary shawl
worn around another body,

invisible, empty of geography,
a bobby pin free from the tumult
of hurt. It carried life within till

pain cracked it open and flowered,
a splendor of sorrow. Now absence
is stitched inside veins, tired tongue

licking the wound close,
an animal moment of worth.

Body time according to my ovaries

is somewhat fluid & fails to run by any known
clock. Instead, it strikes at its own convenience.

I have told my friend, Raluca, my ovaries are fast
to set free the eggs. Earlier each month, as if sweeping

out the old to make space for what's ahead. She
nodded, a shared tenderness in her eyes. All these

b words we accommodate each month: bloaty,
bleeding, bitchy, a metronome of the female syntax.

The depletion of the egg informs the texture of my days,
their poppy pod ripeness or the draining thin limbs.

An animal in limbo: sheer want, self-doubt bouts, mood
swings. Days that feel glued together, body sedated

by uterine power, throbbing and twitching under the
gaze of the ovum. The way she touches my hand.

Self-medicating with St. John's wort

This is youish, says the man, his finger drawing on my
wrist. My skin instantly tingles altogether. He pulls back,
watery eyes glued to my face. Stomach shrinks, nausea
fills up the nostrils, tongue numb with bile. I cling to a shred

of a braced smile. The finger goes up the forearm, prodding
the little scar I got that July I turned eight, falling into the cut
wheat stems, mapping the arm, round the ball of the shoulder,
slithering along the sweaty neck, past jawline, pushing its way

between the tight lips. Smudging the bitter taste along the braces,
nails scratching the inside, against the pink rubber bands.
In the bathroom, I brush my teeth until gums taste metal, neon
light buzzing in my brain. Years later, burning lips and mouth

numb with tea, becomes a high in the truncated days, nowhere
to hide the piles of dead St John's flowers in the brass teapot.

Mal de peau

I dreamed him and there he was,
untroubled, like that late summer,

when we met, in the middle of living
our lives. He looked at me, unhurt eyes,

I almost whispered his name, then somehow
knew words might chase away the vision.

Inside my heart, the name roared
like a famished beast wedged into the flesh.

On my lips, an unborn smile, a moan.
Around us, the world unraveled at full speed.

His eyes lingered on my face and I felt old,
some stranger that couldn't make them gleam

or even blink. The name itched in my throat,
black birds covered the washed-out sky,

some decorum of ambush. He walked past me.
Little deaths camouflaged as honest dreams.

Some Kind of Love

Day's seams

Mornings happen anyways.
Through the open window,
a spell of breeze, and then
an eruption of wings.
My ear finds your chest,
then the dip of your neck
where flakes of fleur de sel
inhabit my lips.
Some fine-grained making.
All my dreams lay folded
into paper planes.

That day

you took me to the Japanese place on South Hope

Street where you ordered to impress and fed me

spicy tofu bites with your chopsticks, asked the waiter

to bring me a fork, she is Romanian, then told me

how you sold cherries with your grandma every summer

back home and your mom begged you to help your cousin

move to LA, then gave a sideways nod to hide your eyes,

the roof of my mouth was on fire, the dim light fell

on your lilac shirt and I gasped for air, the clock

on the wall chimed, more people came in, clouded

in a wisp of tobacco and later, you smoked, then opened

the hotel room to let it breath and I pulled the blanket

up to chin and tried to seem as together as possible,

I was still lumped in places, did you find me linear enough

like twenty years ago, smoke floated like ghost breath

and you kept quiet as my ear rested on your sternum,

there was no heartbeat, instead blood flooding every cell,

behind the glass windows, tiny glows punctured the dark

and I knew you'd done many things, soft and hard,

and folded into yourself for days, watched the sun move,

then still while I craved this burning in the chest, my ears

to buzz a little, nostrils numb with familiar scent, yet the world

tumble dried every inch of memory and now all cuts oozed

with chlorinated light, and the ghosts of our hearts shared a front seat.

Some morning unease

You slip into my mind,

a sort of urgency, defining my pace,

invalidating previous sureness.

Like it's on my list today

not to think of you,

work with my Bridges student

overcome co-dependence,

teach research strategies

in my composition class,

attend a poetry reading in the Village.

But you seem seared

into the circuits of my brain,

quick at semaphoring your presence

when the Starbucks kid rolls the r

in my name, or the man on the steps

of The Met lights up a cigarette

under his breath. It could be

my inner ear craves an unknown tune

of familiar lyrics or the whisper

of a disappearing body. All these details

quicken their spurring as my day unfolds.

Ghost hum filling the air.

How to say hello/goodbye to old love

You text me in the middle of my English class
clumsy with words, eager to spur disaster.
Your words reek of loneliness. An 18-year-old déjà vu.
Nothing feels the same, yet there is a familiar tinge
to your every syllable. It pounds in my sweaty armpits
and echoes in the humming of the AC.
I find myself debating the absence,
then welcoming the presence.
The room shrinks like an old itchy sweater.
Somewhere in the holes,
the raw of your punctured heart
is infecting my Huawei screen.
I got a tattoo you'll never see, two freckled kids
and morning kisses on my sunburnt collarbone.
Your gaze still not wide enough to hold me.
Yet, a million thrills rise in the stuffy air,
giddy with anticipation. No urgency for speech remains.

What scratches inside a thing?

Love is twofold. The burning taste of new,
and the slow, steady work of revision.
At the kitchen table, stitching back
former selves. The familiar gesture
of putting saliva on a ladder down
the pantyhose. Then, a drop of nail polish
to preserve the elusive. Your eyes
measuring the gesture, eager to dismiss.
Later, sewing the running hole, needle's
eye too wide to contain the remains of the day.
Outside, the hungry moon softly cuddling
behind clouds. Its breath, a lungful of summer.

Inside, the heart, a rhizomatic sponge,
flurrier particles going in and out.

Some kind of love

He calls me his stanza.
Words that peel off napkins,
Chase statements, proforma invoices,
occasionally resting on his lips,
as he sips whiskey and water
at wee hours. Undone.
Before the day rolls its million eyes
on his weary face, he randomly pares down
flecks of his heart into fervid words.
The stanza buds like sweet tobacco,
moon still stationed outside the tall window,
music filling the ash-smeared walls.
The pen crushes the fullness of the paper,
its squeaky nib running rivers on my skin.
He tells me suffering is the gateway.

Impermanence

A man reads braille on your ribs, fingertips
soaking in flesh. His face, a splintered sun.

He will make you coffee in the years to come
and not once, scorch your ruffled lips.

He'll keep you alive, walks on crunchy mollusk
shells, listen how they gorge inside your mouth.

He'll teach your son to cup tadpoles with bare hands,
call you limp fish yourselves. Later, summer asphalt

under the feet, will draw a gaping-bird road ahead.
Overnight, ghosts shall return, a polished torture.

When I look up, there he is, thrusting his arm
through the twinned chambers of my heart,

resurfacing within the lustered geometry
of a belated snowflake. Snow smelling sessions.

Greek morning

Breakfast, a hurried affair.
Winding down the narrow streets
of Limenas to buy cheese koulouri,
fresh from the oven,
sesame seeds on my lap,
in your beard,
washing off the numbness
of the tongue with cheap coffee
from the same paper cup.
Outside the window,
oleander bushes and orange trees
carrying their pretty burden in silence.
Where do lost intimacies go?
The thin space where they breathe,
the pale line of the Hellenic skies,
into the soft fragrance
of these unfamiliar days. The mid-air.
Things done with ease.
You say we are unapologetic
in the way we accumulate joy
and loss alike.

My tongue is tied from burn,
and heavy words.
A finger's width of pain.
Still, we stand, morning breeze
cooling the roof of our mouths,
one heart, the size of Thassos.

Dream[e]scape

The shrunken footprint of this strange summer, a tiny slip of a cloud up the July skies. Folding longing into itself. Hear the sea house crinkle with silence, your own heart, an Ikea light fixture. To be held in every jar of home preserved beetle. At night, angst wafts through the heating ducts, pregnant with steamy breath. A three-wheeled vehicle of discontent.

Après angelectomy

Alice Fulton wants me to keep vigil,
never lose sight of the way comfort
strikes one numb, immune to umph
and ready to turn inwards, pupa like.
What keeps my angel from lying
down on the asphalt of the dark
highway and be run down by some
tractor trailer truck? A nexus of love,
tying my weakness to its strength,
both bodies under siege. He wants
to remove himself from my head,
or is it heart? Never mind, I say,
you'll make a sober butterfly, just
follow the trail of the primed blade.

To the man who promised me breakfast

the best pastel de Belém in Belém before we
rode Tram 28 to the torre or later wandered
the flea market, making out in a foreign crowd.
I would let you hold my hand, sticky from pastry
and dusty from fingering the antiques, and get
lost in your thoughts, the way you want me to,
before you whisper ești o frumușică in my left ear
which is always funny, a nineteen-forty movie line
and you won't get the joke because you are more
into theater plays, never watched Bringing Up
Baby breathlessly on Cinemateca nights, on the old
couch in your parents' two-room apartment, though
you lived in the same neighborhood and for sure
pulled my ponytails as we strode in pairs to the
school entrance, cravate roșii around our thin necks.
Did you call me pretty back then or simply smirked
in triumph at my frowned face? You kind of remind
me of the goonie who lost his student badge every week,
never got a nice, short haircut and brought the wrong
Nichita Stănescu poem to read in front of the classmates.
How many women were told they were pretty in Lisbon
as they sipped wine and ate pastéis de bacalhau at Casa
Portuguesa, then were kissed on lips smeared with Serra
da Estralla? Back home, you swear you bought me a small
watermelon from the market in Ostroveni before you
dropped me in front of the apartment building that had

the name of a temperature reading on a glass thermometer.
Isn't it funny how we remember the best versions of ourselves,
or maybe it is the most accommodating ones that we keep
sketching into our minds. Across the bay, sun crashes into sea.

Some things will end for sure

on their own, skin glowed and frail,
the size of mica flakes. A wild flip

of the head, moon caught up in a net
of stars, green eyes warming up skin,

kiss the cheek, wipe the mark kind of
days, blooming scars, washes of cold

through the veins, unlived life throbs,
washed down whispers of you. Other

things will sunder in ash and dust, the
blazing eyes of hurt will find fissures

and occupy them, germinating more
grief and then, could we word build

ourselves anew? This love, a contagion,
yet all we ever knew, will stand still.

Acknowledgements

Grateful acknowledgement is made to the editors of the following journals, in which variations of these poems originally appeared:

A Glimpse Of: 'Quarantine love'

As Above So Below: 'Prayer with lullaby eyes'

Belle Ombre: 'How to turn poetry prompt # 5 into girl power', 'Camera obscura'

Biscuit Root Drive: 'Anatomy of a single sun's day'

Burning House Press: 'In the suburbs', 'Called by others to grow upwards'

Dragonfly Magazine: 'That day'

Elephants Never: 'Halves of things'

Emerge Literary Journal: 'Ghostification'

E-ratio Poetry Journal: 'Contretemps'

Eunoia Review: 'Somethings will end for sure', 'Hands have twelve lives', 'Self-medicating with St. John's wort'

Eurolitkrant: 'What occasionally makes sense'

Evocations: 'Under eyelids'

First Literary Review-East: 'Needle threading towards reparation', 'A woman/hood'

Fishbowl Press: 'Three winks', 'The hues of April blues in Long Island'

Fragmented Voices: 'Madrugada'

From the Ashes Womxn Anthology: 'PASS'

Ghost City Press: 'Girlhood Lessons'

Headstuff: 'Day's Seams'

January Review: 'Dear Sugar gives late night advice', 'The twenty-year marriage', 'A revision of the self'

Leon Literary Review: 'To the man who promised me breakfast'

LitArt Hub: 'Ode to the 80s scrapbooks'

Literary Orphans: 'At the villa', 'My therapist asks me to write down ten things my mother loved'

Lumiere Review: 'In undergloom'

Mediterranean Poetry: 'Mal de mer', 'Ars Amandi', 'Dream(e) scape'

Miletus: 'Summer's time', 'Greek morning'

Pirene's Fountain, Volume 14, Issue 22: 'Portrait of my mother in the middle of things'

Poetry Magazine: 'Confession'

Remington Review: 'Band aid'

Rogue Agent: 'Body time according to my ovaries'

Santa Ana River Review: 'What scratches inside a thing?'

Stonecrop Magazine: 'How to say hello/goodbye to old love'

Tempered Runes Press: 'Of forgotten tastes'

The Big Window Review: 'A day spent curled around your face', 'To the god on watch'

The Blue Nib: 'Limenas, half-light'

The Kindling Journal: 'Some morning unease'

The Inverse Journal: 'What makes a girl'

The Night Heron Barks: 'Mal de peau'

The Raven Review: 'Impermanence'

The Stray Branch: 'A poem about things I became good at losing'

Trouvaille Review: 'Complicities'

Wax International: 'White-night odes'

Witches Magazine: 'Mothering'

WordCity Monthly: 'Ambience of elsewhere', 'I haven't thought about my mother in months', 'A tincture for wounds'

45 Magazine: 'Some kind of love'

14 Magazine: 'Après angelectomy'

Notes:

oracole – scrapbooks

multiubitul tovarăş -our beloved comrade (accepted manner of addressing Nicolae Ceauşescu during the Romanian communist regime)

cravate roşii –red neckties (worn by every child during the Romanian communist regime)

fori, fete, filme sau băieţi -an outdoor socializing games for elder children based on the idea of competing choices

nechezol – coffee substitute imposed on the market in the last years of communism in Romania

Scînteia -The Spark, the press organ of the Romanian Communist Party

ostropel de pui cu mămăliguţă, pastramă, albă-ca-zăpadă, salată de vinete -Romanian dishes

must -grape juice

afumătoare -smokehouse

orez cu lapte -rice with milk

eşti o frumuşică -you are pretty

Cinemateca -name of a 1980 movie program on the Romanian television

Nichita Stănescu -Romanian poet, writer and essayist

Ostroveni- neighborhood in Rm. Vâlcea, Romania

Lightning Source UK Ltd.
Milton Keynes UK
UKHW020635271021
392924UK00012B/774